CLASSIC GUITAR Adapted by **Bill Purse**

MEL BAY PRESENTS
BACH CHORALES FOR GUITAR

For Solo, Duet, Trio, or Quartet.

Preface by Dr. Aaron Shearer

EDITIONES CLASSICAE

A stereo cassette tape as well as standard MIDI sequencer files of the music in this book are now available. The publisher strongly recommends the use of the cassette tape or MIDI files to insure accuracy of interpretation and ease in learning. See page 215 of this book for order form.

Contents

Preface by Aaron Shearer

This book is a gold mine of study material for a wide range of guitar students who seek to improve their ability to read music on the guitar while enjoying the process. But both the improvement and enjoyment depend entirely upon the individual's approach to study.

During practice it's essential to be acutely aware that you're forming habits which will dictate how you play. Unavoidably, if you build habits of confusion and error in practice, confusion and error will occur when you perform. So for the greatest reward and enjoyment from the study of this appealing music, proceed carefully and with caution.

Reading and performing music requires the ability to read ahead before playing and to decide the location of notes on the fingerboard, the fingering, and rhythm. On more advanced levels, this process includes determining expressive groupings and overall interpretation. The similarity between this activity and reading a story or poem aloud has often been pointed out.

Obviously reading and playing music is a complex endeavor requiring a great deal of careful study and practice—as well as patience. To avoid habits of confusion and error this endeavor must be approached in a progressive, step-by-step manner. An important early step is **pre-reading***.

Pre-reading is carried out away from the guitar and is a systematic way to approach playing without confusion and error. By solving problems before you actually play, you're doing essentially what proficient readers do at sight. The difference is in how quickly you do it; well-trained sight-readers read ahead, deciding as they play. Since you're still developing the ability to sightread, you'll solve problems more slowly and deliberately. By working slowly and deliberately now, you'll build habits which will eventually enable you to sightread accurately and confidently. Thus, pre-fluent sightreading.

Pre-reading involves visualization*, and visualization is the key to minimizing confusion and error. Visualization means reading the music away from the guitar—seeing and feeling the music unfold under your fingers as though you were actually playing it on the guitar. The purpose of visualization is to ensure that you clearly understand the music before you play.

Proceed as follows:

Select a single, double, or three-voice part which you consider practical for your level of ability, that is, which you can approach without confusion and error.

♪ Choose a slow, safe tempo and visualize that part as though you were playing it on the guitar. If the material appears to be a problem in fingering or execution, that part is probably too difficult for your sightreading training. You should select a less challenging part and proceed to visualize it until fluent.

♪ When you can confidently visualize the material without hesitation at a reasonable effective tempo, play it on the guitar, being careful not to pause. If you become confused and must pause, you didn't visualize the material sufficiently. Re-visualize the problem passage and then play.

♪ When you can play your part alone securely and without hesitation, you're ready to enjoy performing this beautiful music with others or with the recordings.

Dr. Aaron Shearer

Aaron Shearer

Duquesne University

*The concepts of pre-reading and visualization are more thoroughly explained in my *Learning the Classic Guitar, Part Two,* published by Mel Bay Publications, Inc. See page 214 for detailed information.

Foreword by Joe Negri

Throughout history the guitar has been the instrument of choice for free-spirited individuals seeking freedom of expression. The concept of adventure and "romance" have played a dominant role in the guitar's growth and development. Because of its "portable" nature, the guitar has never become "staid" or "proper" in the Victorian sense. In fact the guitar has been looked upon as somewhat of a rebel in the family of musical instruments. I grant you this exciting past has been responsible for much of the charm and uniqueness of this small wooden box that Berlioz called a "miniature orchestra."

However, the guitar's volatile and nomadic history has seriously deterred development of guitar pedagogy. Despite the tremendous advances made in the last decade or so, the guitar still is woefully behind in methodology when compared to other musical instruments. Today's music stores are inundated with material for guitar, but that wasn't always the case. I can recall as a student not too long ago, the severe lack of guitar methods and study books. I'm speaking here specifically about Plectrum/Jazz guitar. All of this has seriously handicapped the development of guitarists. Guitar players don't develop along conventional lines that most instrumentalists do. We (guitarists) have always had a serious hang-up with musical notation. It's something that most guitarists are not proud of. But, it is a "fact of life" guitarists are "notoriously bad music readers." We all secretly envy the reading skills of pianists, horn players, string players, whatever!

If you can identify with this situation then you will truly appreciate the collection of chorales that Bill Purse has compiled. You can develop your reading skills to accommodate whatever level you may be on. Starting with long tones and simple rhythms to double stops and chords—to more complex rhythm figures; this book has it all. Reading often has been described as a "necessary evil." Well Mr. Purse has tamed the savage beast. Now you can practice your reading and make beautiful music at the same time.

Happy Reading!

Joe Negri

Joe Negri

Introduction by Bill Purse

Guitarists have long been in need of sightreading exercises suitable to many skill levels. After searching in vain for suitable material for my students, I decided to adapt the Bach Chorales frequently used for sightreading by piano students. This two-volume series is a result of my efforts to create a flexible system of sightreading studies for guitarists in chordal form, covering the full range of the guitar and all key signatures, both major and relative minor.

About the Arrangements

Each of thirty-four traditional Bach Chorales is presented in the following forms:

♪ Quartets: each voice may be assigned to one of four guitarists for an ensemble study.

♪ Trios: by combining the alto and tenor voices into one part, the chorales may be performed by three guitarists.

♪ Duets: three different combinations of the four voices yield a variety of duets.

> Balanced duets combine the soprano and alto voices for part one and the tenor and bass voices for part two.
> Melody studies feature the soprano voice supported by the combined lower voices played by the second part. (Melody studies also make wonderful flute and guitar studies at octave written or *8vb.*)
> Bass studies feature the bass voice supported by the combined upper voices played as the second part.

♪ Solo: the four voices are combined into a solo arrangement using traditional classical guitar technique, or plectrum and fingers.

Fingerings are not included, so as to allow the guitarist to develop fingerings in multiple positions and allow greater focus on only the pitch component of sightreading.

Using the Arrangements

Students may proceed in any order throughout this text, approaching pieces in several ways. The half-note values may be augmented to whole notes, if necessary, for continuity between chord voicings. Teachers should have their students analyze the harmonic progressions of Bach, paying particular attention to his extraordinary voice leading. Try adding passing tones and ornamentation to the studies for improvisational practice. The chorales in this edition make exceptional warm-up studies for guitar ensemble practice. This book can be utilized with guitarists at any skill level, depending on which arrangements are used and the assignment of student and teacher parts.

Using MIDI

When performing with the cassette or sequences, the fermatta (⌢) on half notes will double the time value, while a fermatta over the whole note will be ignored. Standard MIDI sequencer files are available for all thirty-four chorales, and each of the four voices may be auditioned or disabled for playback at any tempo without changing its pitch. The chorale studies may also be used as sight-singing exercises for the guitarist or vocalists by working with a computer or dedicated sequencer. Tracks 1-4 are soprano, alto, tenor, and bass respectively. Track 5 contains a count-off rim shot on Ch. 10. You can re-orchestrate the chorales by inserting whatever patch change numbers you wish. For information concerning purchasing standard MIDI files of the chorales, see page 215.

About the Arranger

Bill Purse is the Chair Guitar and Chair of Music Synthesis at Duquesne University. He received his B.M. in studio performance and his Master's in composition from Duquesne, and has studied privately with Joe Negri, Vic Juris, and Pat Martino. As the author of *Bach Chorales for Guitar* (Mel Bay Publications), and *Basic Guitar Structures,* Bill has pioneered the utilization of interactive MIDI files and music score publication. He has specialized in developing accelerated learning techniques for mastering music notation software, *Introducing Finale 3.0: (A Student's Guide to Shortening the Learning Curve),* as well as for the guitar, including an interactive multi-media software series, *The Guitar Atlas,* for Lyrrus, Inc.

Purse has performed in concert with Al DiMeola, Emily Remler, Joe Pass, Leni Stern, Barney Kessel, Herb Ellis, Larry Carlton, Billy Cobham, and Stanley Clark and has been a featured artist at several arts festivals, including the Three Rivers Arts Festival, Shadyside Jazz Festival, Mellon Jazz Festival, and Westmoreland Arts Festival. In 1993, Purse was the guitarist for the Civic Light Opera production of *Fame.* As a consultant for Fender Musical Instruments and Apple Computer, he is a frequent and well-known lecturer and clinician on guitar synthesis and computer/MIDI applications for the guitar. Purse is a staff writer for *The MIDI Guitarist* and has been featured in articles published in the *Roland Users Guide, Korg Patches, Korg Pro-View, Electronic Musician,* and *Guitar Player* Magazine.

A composer, arranger, and producer in radio and television, he has released and produced several albums of original music, *Time A La Mode, Free, Inside Joke,* and *Catch Twenty-Two Live at Cardillo's.* He has toured the world with the synthesizer ensemble AERGO, and is the musical director, guitarist and arranger for the Duquesne University faculty guitar ensemble CATCH TWENTY-TWO.

Special thanks to Lynn Purse, Dr. Judith Bowman, and Don Tubbs for their help and patience.

Bach Chorale Number 1 (Quartet)
"Oh Treasure Above Treasures"

When playing along with the cassette or MIDI sequences, the fermatta over a half note will double its duration. A fermatta over a whole note will have no change in the note's duration.

Bach Chorale Number 1 (Trio)

"Oh Treasure Above Treasures"

Bach Chorale Number 1 (Duet)

"Oh Treasure Above Treasures"

Bach Chorale Number 1 (Melody)

"Oh Treasure Above Treasures"

Bach Chorale Number 1 (Bass Study)

"Oh Treasure Above Treasures"

Bach Chorale Number 1 (Solo)

"Oh Treasure Above Treasures"

Bach Chorale Number 2 (Quartet)

"From God Shall Naught Divide Me"

Bach Chorale Number 2 (Trio)

"From God Shall Naught Divide Me"

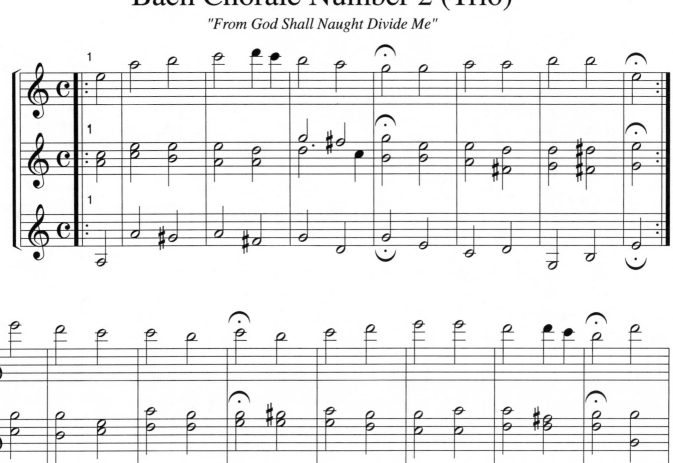

Bach Chorale Number 2 (Duet)

"From God Shall Naught Divide Me"

Bach Chorale Number 2 (Melody)

"From God Shall Naught Divide Me"

Bach Chorale Number 2 (Bass)

"From God Shall Naught Divide Me"

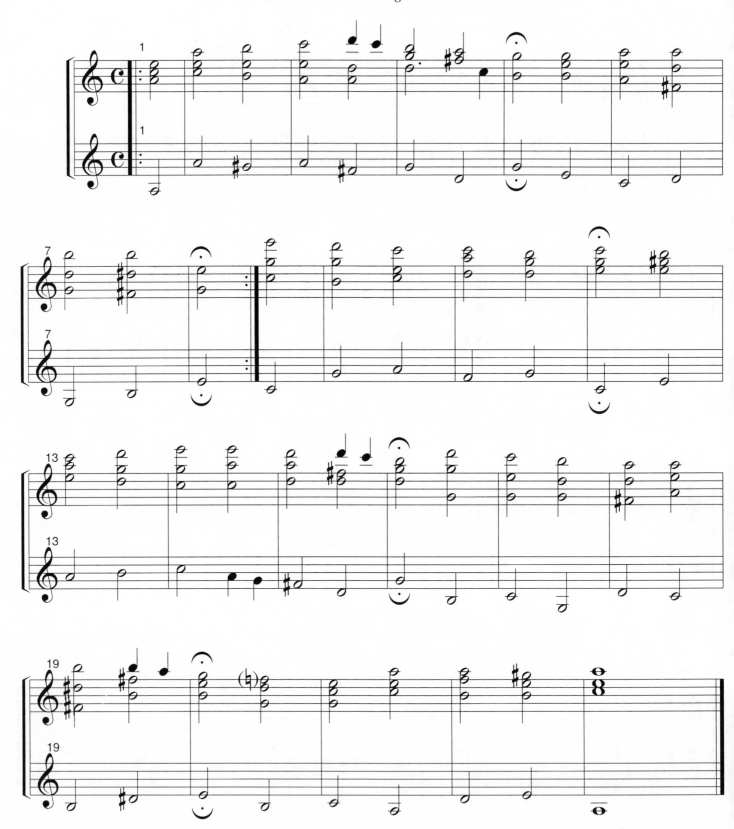

Bach Chorale Number 2 (Solo)

"From God Shall Naught Divide Me"

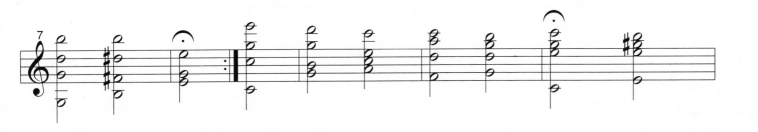

Bach Chorale Number 3 (Quartet)

"Oh My Soul Be Glad And Joyful"

Bach Chorale Number 3 (Trio)

"Oh My Soul Be Glad And Joyful"

Bach Chorale Number 3 (Duet)

"Oh My Soul Be Glad And Joyful"

Bach Chorale Number 3 (Melody Study)

"Oh My Soul Be Glad And Joyful"

Bach Chorale Number 3 (Bass Study)

"Oh My Soul Be Glad And Joyful"

Bach Chorale Number 3 (Solo)

"Oh My Soul Be Glad And Joyful"

Bach Chorale Number 4 (Quartet)

"Oh Wither Shall I Flee"

Bach Chorale Number 4 (Trio)

"Oh Wither Shall I Flee"

Bach Chorale Number 4 (Duet)

"Oh Wither Shall I Flee"

Bach Chorale Number 4 (Melody Study)

"Oh Wither Shall I Flee"

Bach Chorale Number 4 (Bass Study)

"Oh Wither Shall I Flee"

Bach Chorale Number 4 (Solo)

"Oh Wither Shall I Flee"

Bach Chorale Number 5 (Quartet)

"God The Father, Be Our Stay"

Bach Chorale Number 5 (Trio)

"God The Father, Be Our Stay"

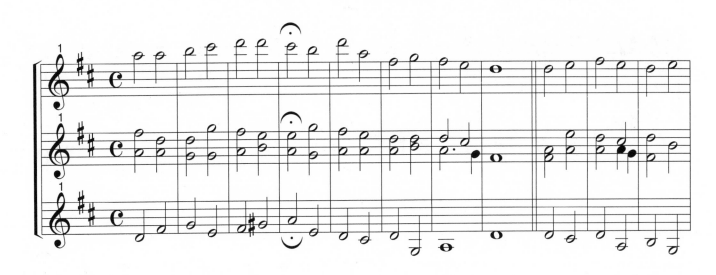

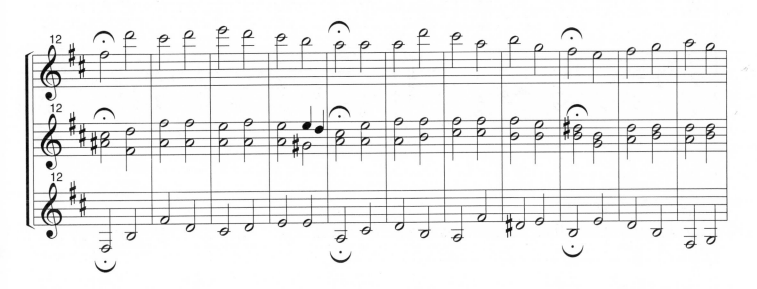

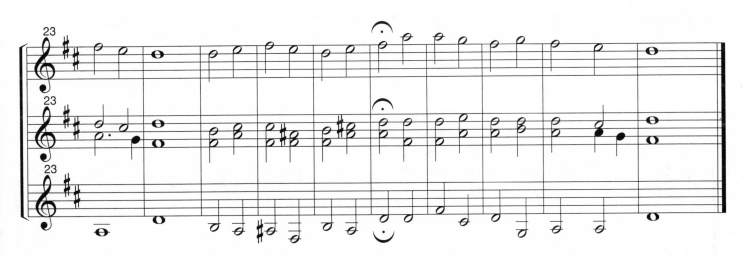

Bach Chorale Number 5 (Duet)

"God The Father, Be Our Stay"

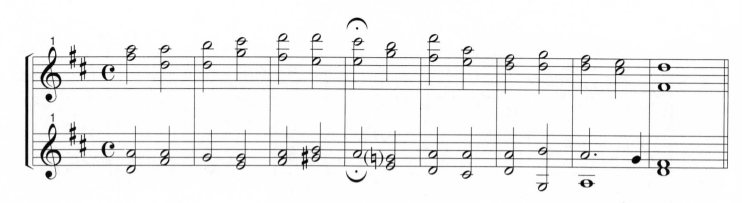

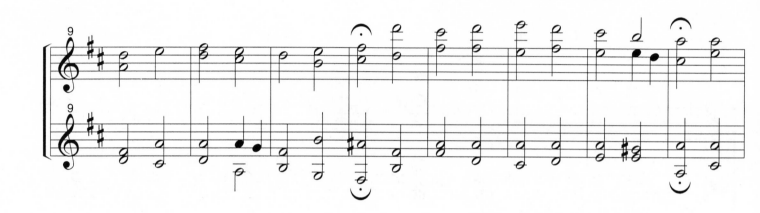

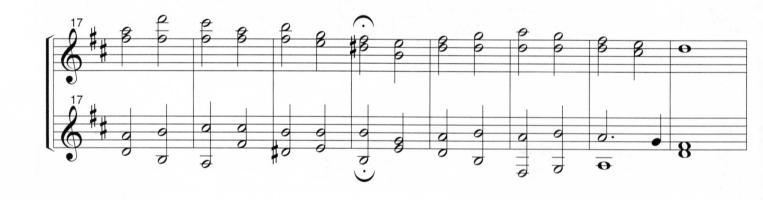

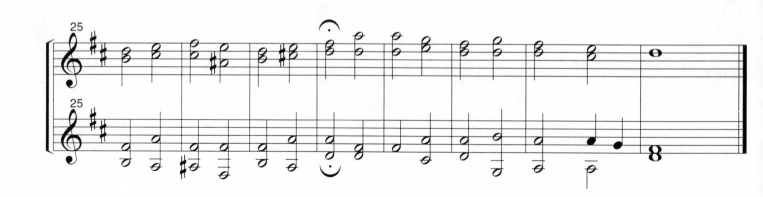

Bach Chorale Number 5 (Melody Study)

"God The Father, Be Our Stay"

Bach Chorale Number 5 (Bass Study)

"God The Father, Be Our Stay"

Bach Chorale Number 5 (Solo)

"God The Father, Be Our Stay"

Bach Chorale Number 6 (Quartet)

"The Will Of God Is Always Best"

Bach Chorale Number 6 (Trio)

"The Will Of God Is Always Best"

Bach Chorale Number 6 (Duet)

"The Will Of God Is Always Best"

Bach Chorale 6 (Melody Study)

"The Will Of God Is Always Best"

Bach Chorale Number 6 (Bass Study)

"The Will Of God Is Always Best"

Bach Chorale Number 6 (Solo)

"The Will Of God Is Always Best"

Bach Chorale Number 7 (Quartet)

"Christ, The Life Of All Living"

Bach Chorale Number 7 (Trio)

"Christ, The Life Of All Living"

Bach Chorale Number 7 (Duet)

"Christ, The Life Of All Living"

Bach Chorale Number 7 (Melody Study)

"Christ, The Life Of All Living"

Bach Chorale Number 7 (Bass Study)

"Christ, The Life Of All Living"

Bach Chorale Number 7 (Solo)

"Christ, The Life Of All Living"

Bach Chorale Number 8 (Quartet)

"God Gave Us This Glorious Day"

Bach Chorale Number 8 (Trio)

"God Gave Us This Glorious Day"

Bach Chorale Number 8 (Duet)

"God Gave Us This Glorious Day"

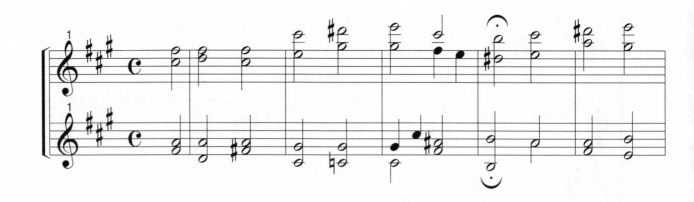

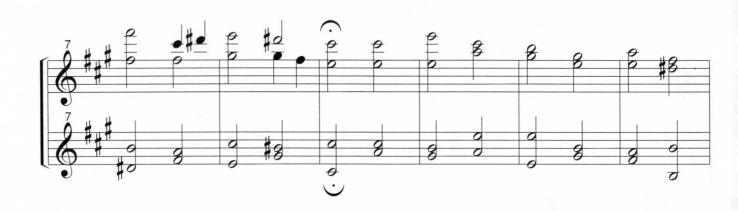

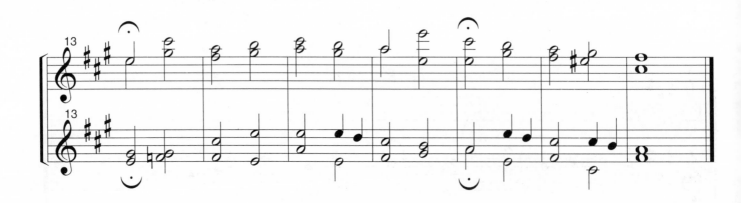

Bach Chorale Number 8 (Melody Study)

"God Gave Us This Glorious Day"

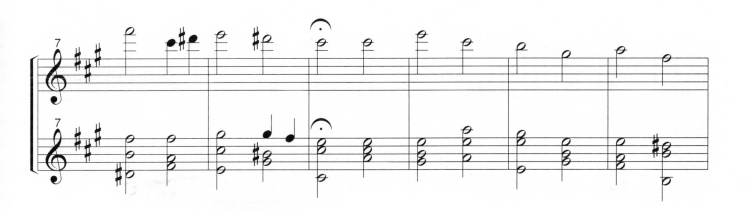

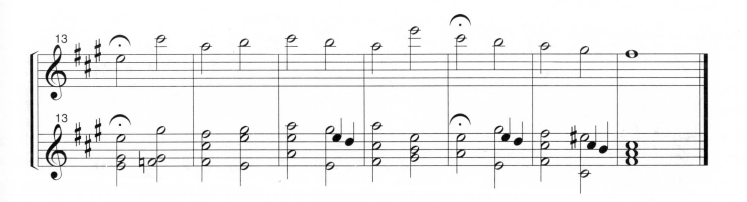

Bach Chorale Number 8 (Bass Study)

"God Gave Us This Glorious Day"

Bach Chorale Number 8 (Solo)

"God Gave Us This Glorious Day"

Bach Chorale Number 9 (Quartet)

"I Know, My Lord, That all My Tasks"

Bach Chorale Number 9 (Trio)

"I Know, My Lord, That all My Tasks"

Bach Chorale Number 9 (Duet)

"I Know, My Lord, That all My Tasks"

Bach Chorale Number 9 (Melody Study)

"I Know, My Lord, That all My Tasks"

Bach Chorale Number 9 (Bass Study)

"I Know, My Lord, That all My Tasks"

Bach Chorale Number 9 (Solo)

"I Know, My Lord, That all My Tasks"

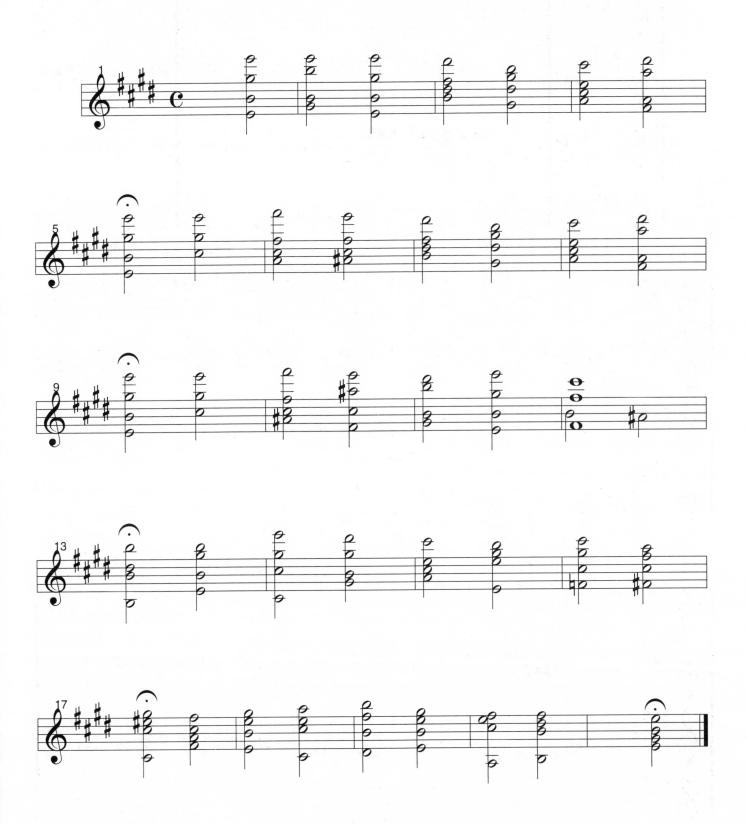

Bach Chorale Number 10 (Quartet)

"Thee We Thank With Hearts And Voices"

Bach Chorale Number 10 (Trio)

"Thee We Thank With Hearts And Voices"

Bach Chorale Number 10 (Duet)

"Thee We Thank With Hearts And Voices"

Bach Chorale Number 10 (Melody Study)

"Thee We Thank With Hearts And Voices"

Bach Chorale Number 10 (Bass Study)

"Thee We Thank With Hearts And Voices"

Bach Chorale Number 10 (Solo)

"Thee We Thank With Hearts And Voices"

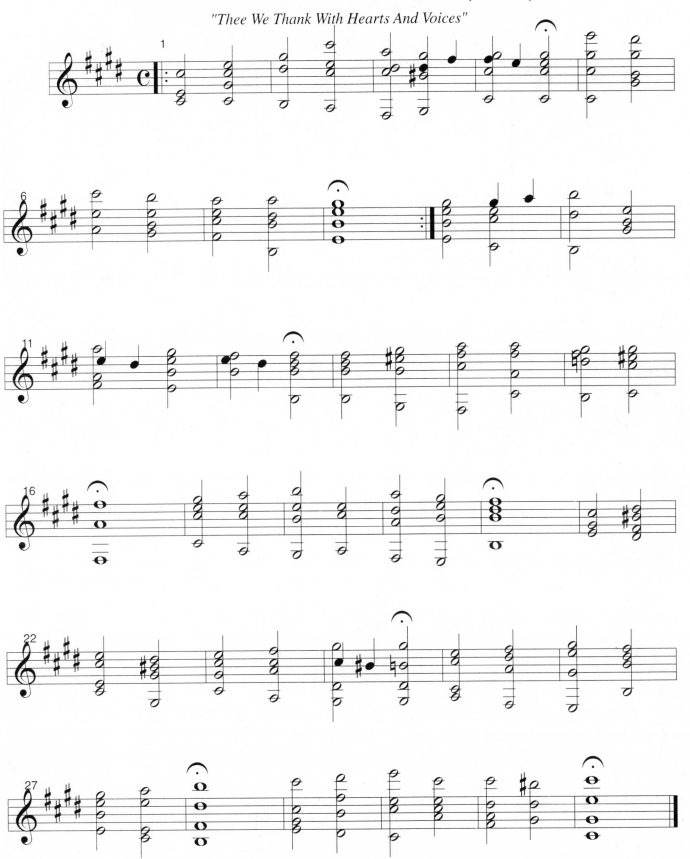

Bach Chorale Number 11 (Quartet)

"I Thank Thee, Precious Savior"

Bach Chorale Number 11 (Trio)

"I Thank Thee, Precious Saviour"

Bach Chorale Number 11 (Duet)

"I Thank Thee, Precious Saviour"

Bach Chorale Number 11 (Melody)

"I Thank Thee, Precious Saviour"

Bach Chorale Number 11 (Bass)

"I Thank Thee, Precious Saviour"

Bach Chorale Number 11 (Solo)

"I Thank Thee, Precious Saviour"

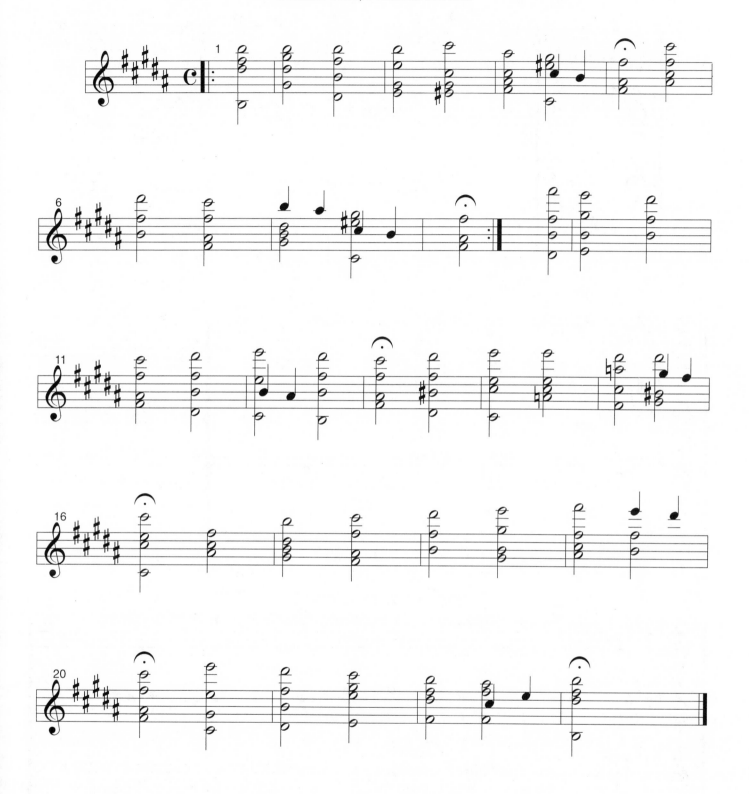

Bach Chorale Number 12 (Quartet)

"If Thou But Suffer God To Guide Thee"

Bach Chorale Number 12 (Trio)

"If Thou But Suffer God To Guide Thee"

Bach Chorale Number 12 (Duet)

"If Thou But Suffer God To Guide Thee"

Bach Chorale Number 12 (Melody)

"If Thou But Suffer God To Guide Thee"

Bach Chorale Number 12 (Bass Study)

"If Thou But Suffer God To Guide Thee"

Bach Chorale Number 12 (Solo)

"If Thou But Suffer God To Guide Thee"

Bach Chorale Number 13 (Quartet)

"Rise Again, Yes, Rise Again With Thou"

Bach Chorale Number 13 (Trio)

"Rise Again, Yes, Rise Again With Thou"

Bach Chorale Number 13 (Duet)

"Rise Again, Yes, Rise Again With Thou"

Bach Chorale Number 13 (Melody Study)

"Rise Again, Yes, Rise Again With Thou"

Bach Chorale Number 13 (Bass Study)

"Rise Again, Yes, Rise Again With Thou"

Bach Chorale Number 13 (Solo)

"Rise Again, Yes, Rise Again With Thou"

Bach Chorale Number 14 (Quartet)

"O, How Blest Are Ye Whose Toils Are Ended"

Bach Chorale Number 14 (Trio)

"O, How Blest Are Ye Whose Toils Are Ended"

Bach Chorale Number 14 (Duet)

"O, How Blest Are Ye Whose Toils Are Ended"

Bach Chorale Number 14 (Melody Study)

"O, How Blest Are Ye Whose Toils Are Ended"

Bach Chorale Number 14 (Bass Study)

"O, How Blest Are Ye Whose Toils Are Ended"

Bach Chorale Number 14 (Solo)

"O, How Blest Are Ye Whose Toils Are Ended"

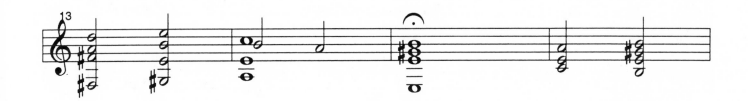

Bach Chorale Number 15 (Quartet)

"God Liveth Yet; Soul, Why Despair And Fret?"

Bach Chorale Number 15 (Trio)

"God Liveth Yet; Soul, Why Despair And Fret?"

Bach Chorale Number 15 (Duet)

"God Liveth Yet; Soul, Why Despair And Fret?"

Bach Chorale Number 15 (Melody Study)

"God Liveth Yet; Soul, Why Despair And Fret?"

Bach Chorale Number 15 (Bass Study)

"God Liveth Yet; Soul, Why Despair And Fret?"

Bach Chorale Number 15 (Solo)

"God Liveth Yet; Soul, Why Despair And Fret?"

97

Bach Chorale Number 16 (Quartet)

"Jesus, Priceless Treasure"

Bach Chorale Number 16 (Trio)

"Jesus, Priceless Treasure"

Bach Chorale Number 16 (Duet)

"Jesus, Priceless Treasure"

Bach Chorale Number 16 (Melody Study)

"Jesus, Priceless Treasure"

Bach Chorale Number 16 (Bass Study)

"Jesus, Priceless Treasure"

Bach Chorale Number 16 (Solo)

"Jesus, Priceless Treasure"

Bach Chorale Number 17 (Quartet)

"The Heav'ns Declare To Us God's Endless Glory"

Bach Chorale Number 17 (Trio)

"The Heav'ns Declare To Us God's Endless Glory"

Bach Chorale Number 17 (Duet)

"The Heav'ns Declare To Us God's Endless Glory"

Bach Chorale Number 17 (Melody Study)

"The Heav'ns Declare To Us God's Endless Glory"

Bach Chorale Number 17 (Bass Study)

"The Heav'ns Declare To Us God's Endless Glory"

Bach Chorale Number 17 (Solo)

"The Heav'ns Declare To Us God's Endless Glory"

Bach Chorale Number 18 (Quartet)

"Sunshine Rays Dispel The Fog"

Bach Chorale Number 18 (Trio)

"Sunshine Rays Dispel The Fog"

Bach Chorale Number 18 (Duet)

"Sunshine Rays Dispel The Fog"

Bach Chorale Number 18 (Melody Study)

"Sunshine Rays Dispel The Fog"

Bach Chorale Number 18 (Bass Study)

"Sunshine Rays Dispel The Fog"

Bach Chorale Number 18 (Solo)

"Sunshine Rays Dispel The Fog"

Bach Chorale Number 19 (Quartet)

"Soul, Adorn Thyself With Gladness"

Bach Chorale Number 19 (Trio)

"Soul, Adorn Thyself With Gladness"

Bach Chorale Number 19 (Duet)

"Soul, Adorn Thyself With Gladness"

118

Bach Chorale Number 19 (Melody Study)

"Soul, Adorn Thyself With Gladness"

Bach Chorale Number 19 (Bass Study)

"Soul, Adorn Thyself With Gladness"

Bach Chorale Number 19 (Solo)

"Soul, Adorn Thyself With Gladness"

Bach Chorale Number 20 (Quartet)
"My Heart Is Filled With Longing"

Bach Chorale Number 20 (Trio)

"My Heart Is Filled With Longing"

Bach Chorale Number 20 (Duet)

"My Heart Is Filled With Longing"

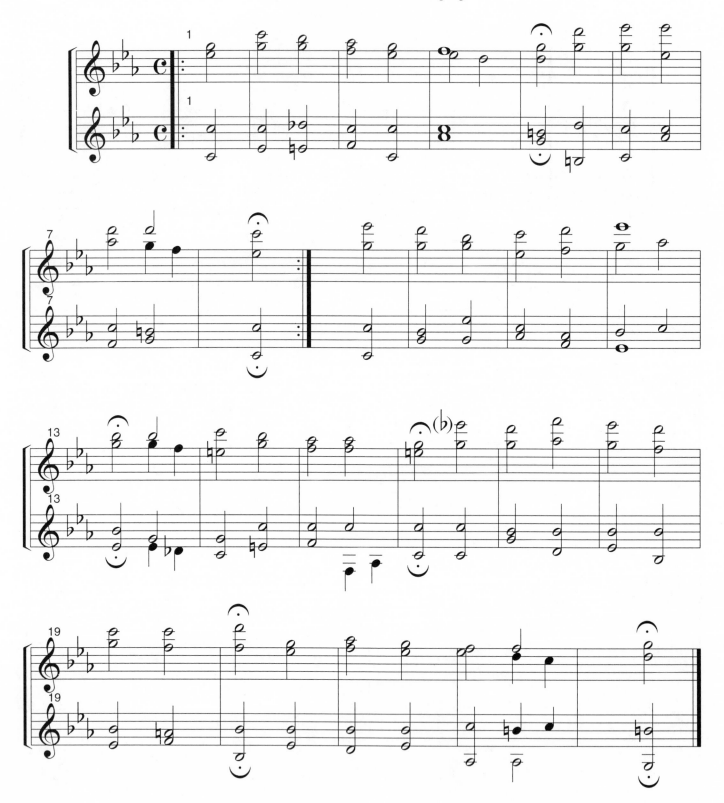

Bach Chorale Number 20 (Melody Study)

"My Heart Is Filled With Longing"

Bach Chorale Number 20 (Bass Study)

"My Heart Is Filled With Longing"

Bach Chorale Number 20 (Solo)

"My Heart Is Filled With Longing"

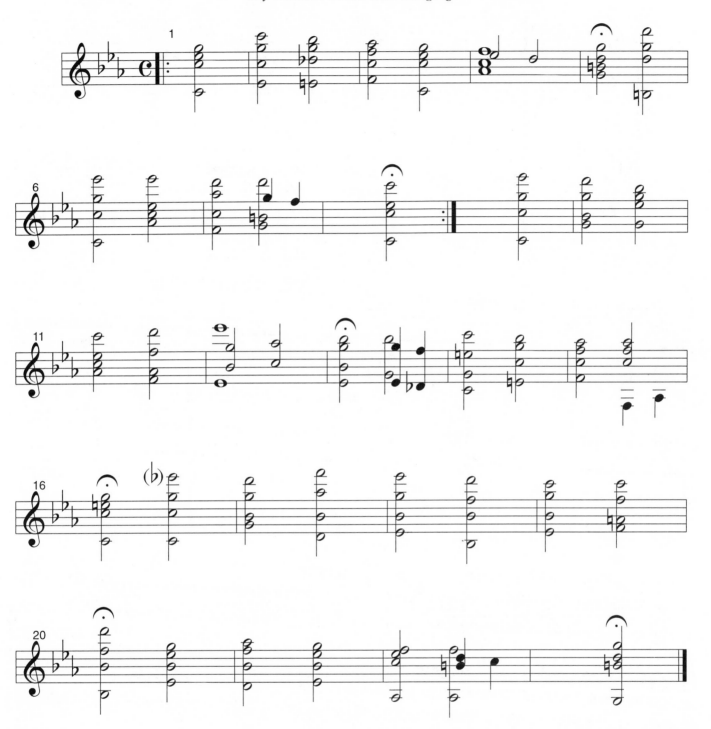

Bach Chorale Number 21 (Quartet)

"Show Forth Your Faith In God Eternal"

Bach Chorale Number 21 (Trio)

"Show Forth Your Faith In God Eternal"

Bach Chorale Number 21 (Duet)

"Show Forth Your Faith In God Eternal"

Bach Chorale Number 21 (Melody Study)

"Show Forth Your Faith In God Eternal"

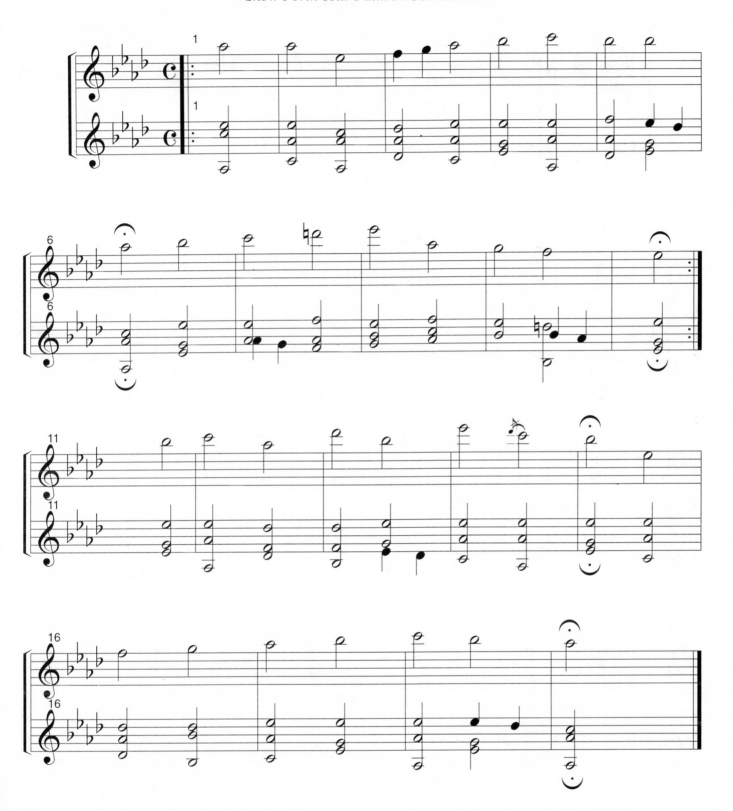

Bach Chorale Number 21 (Bass Study)

"Show Forth Your Faith In God Eternal"

Bach Chorale Number 21 (Solo)

"Show Forth Your Faith In God Eternal"

Bach Chorale Number 22 (Quartet)

"What Shall I, A Sinner, Do, Lord"

Bach Chorale Number 22 (Trio)

"What Shall I, A Sinner, Do, Lord"

Bach Chorale Number 22 (Duet)

"What Shall I, A Sinner, Do, Lord"

Bach Chorale Number 22 (Melody Study)

What Shall I, A Sinner, Do, Lord"

Bach Chorale Number 22 (Bass Study)

"What Shall I, A Sinner, Do, Lord"

Bach Chorale Number 22 (Solo)

"What Shall I, A Sinner, Do, Lord"

Bach Chorale Number 23 (Quartet)

"God The Father, Be Our Stay"

Bach Chorale Number 23 (Trio)

"God The Father, Be Our Stay"

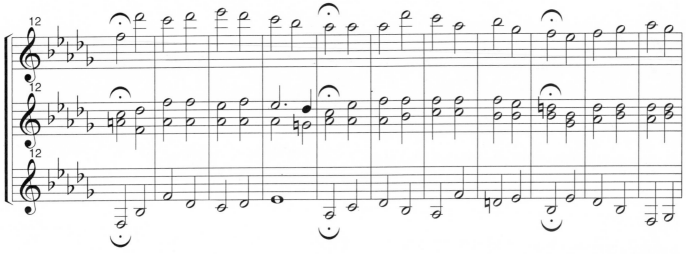

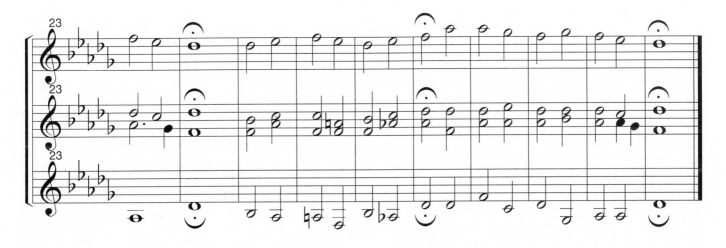

Bach Chorale Number 23 (Duet)

"God The Father, Be Our Stay"

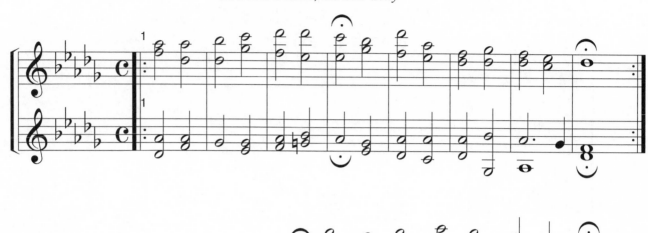

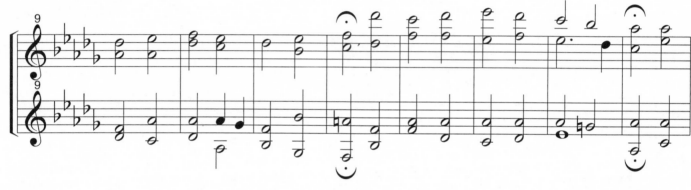

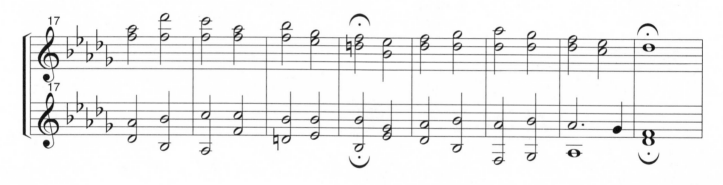

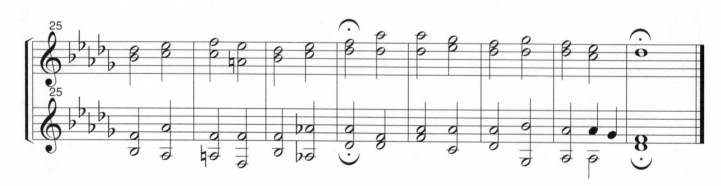

Bach Chorale Number 23 (Melody Study)

"God The Father, Be Our Stay"

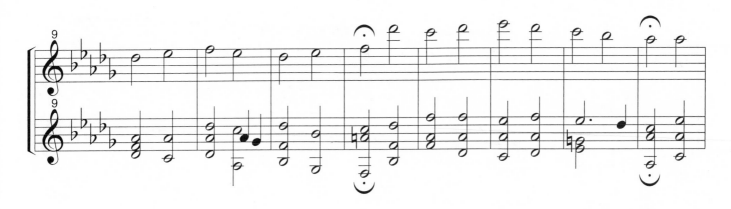

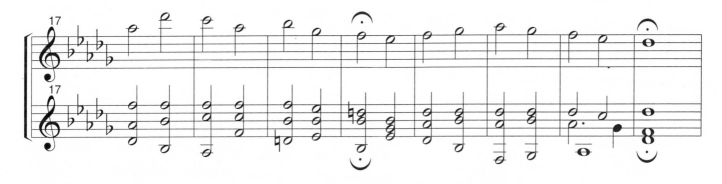

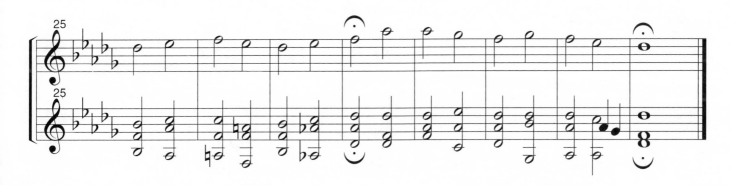

Bach Chorale Number 23 (Bass Study)

"God The Father, Be Our Stay"

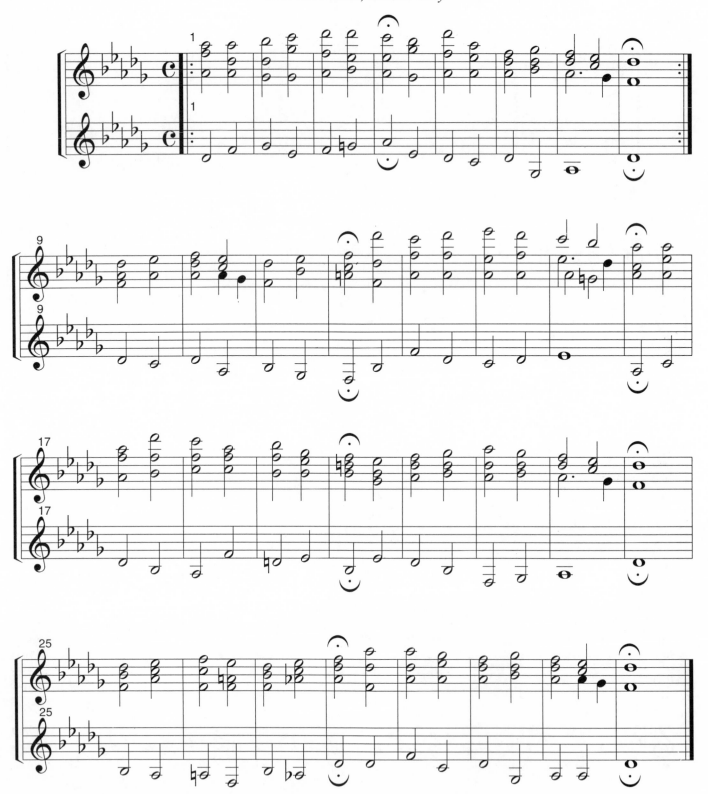

Bach Chorale Number 23 (Solo)

"God The Father, Be Our Stay"

Bach Chorale Number 24 (Quartet)

"Lord, To Thee I Make Confession"

Bach Chorale Number 24 (Trio)

"Lord, To Thee I Make Confession"

Bach Chorale Number 24 (Duet)

"Lord, To Thee I Make Confession"

Bach Chorale Number 24 (Melody Study)

"Lord, To Thee I Make Confession"

Bach Chorale Number 24 (Bass Study)

"Lord, To Thee I Make Confession"

Bach Chorale Number 24 (Solo)

"Lord, To Thee I Make Confession"

Bach Chorale Number 25 (Quartet)
"Jehovah, Let Me Now Adore Thee"

Bach Chorale Number 25 (Trio)

"Jehovah, Let Me Now Adore Thee"

Bach Chorale Number 25 (Duet)

"Jehovah, Let Me Now Adore Thee"

Bach Chorale Number 25 (Melody Study)

"Jehovah, Let Me Now Adore Thee"

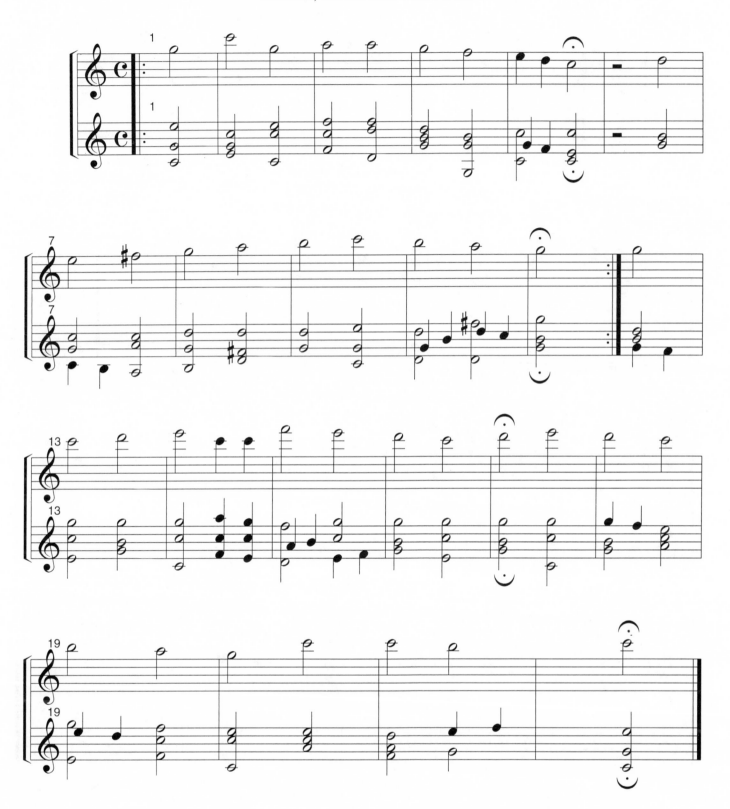

Bach Chorale Number 25 (Bass Study)

"Jehovah, Let Me Now Adore Thee"

Bach Chorale Number 25 (Solo)

"Jehovah, Let Me Now Adore Thee"

Bach Chorale Number 26 (Quartet)

"All Mankind Fell In Adam's Fall"

Bach Chorale Number 26 (Trio)

"All Mankind Fell In Adam's Fall"

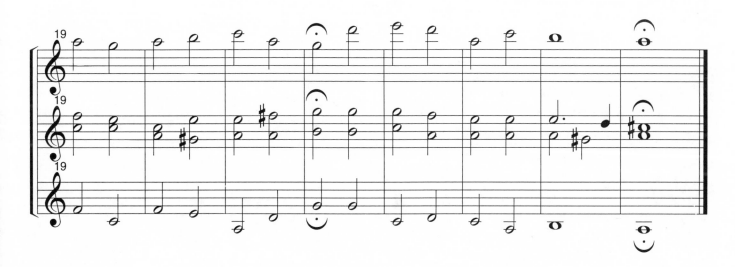

Bach Chorale Number 26 (Duet)

"All Mankind Fell In Adam's Fall"

Bach Chorale Number 26 (Melody Study)

"All Mankind Fell In Adam's Fall"

Bach Chorale Number 26 (Bass Study)

"All Mankind Fell In Adam's Fall"

Bach Chorale Number 26 (Solo)

"All Mankind Fell In Adam's Fall"

Bach Chorale Number 27 (Quartet)

"Whate'er The Task Before Me"

Bach Chorale Number 27 (Trio)

"Whate'er The Task Before Me"

Bach Chorale Number 27 (Duet)

"Whate'er The Task Before Me"

Bach Chorale Number 27 (Melody Study)

"Whate'er The Task Before Me"

Bach Chorale Number 27 (Bass Study)

"Whate'er The Task Before Me"

168

Bach Chorale Number 27 (Solo)

"Whate'er The Task Before Me"

Bach Chorale Number 28 (Quartet)
"Savior Of The Nations, Come"

Bach Chorale Number 28 (Trio)

"Savior Of The Nations, Come"

Bach Chorale Number 28 (Duet)

"Savior Of The Nations, Come"

Bach Chorale Number 28 (Melody Study)

"Savior Of The Nations, Come"

Bach Chorale Number 28 (Bass Study)

"Savior Of The Nations, Come"

Bach Chorale Number 28 (Solo)

"Savior Of The Nations, Come"

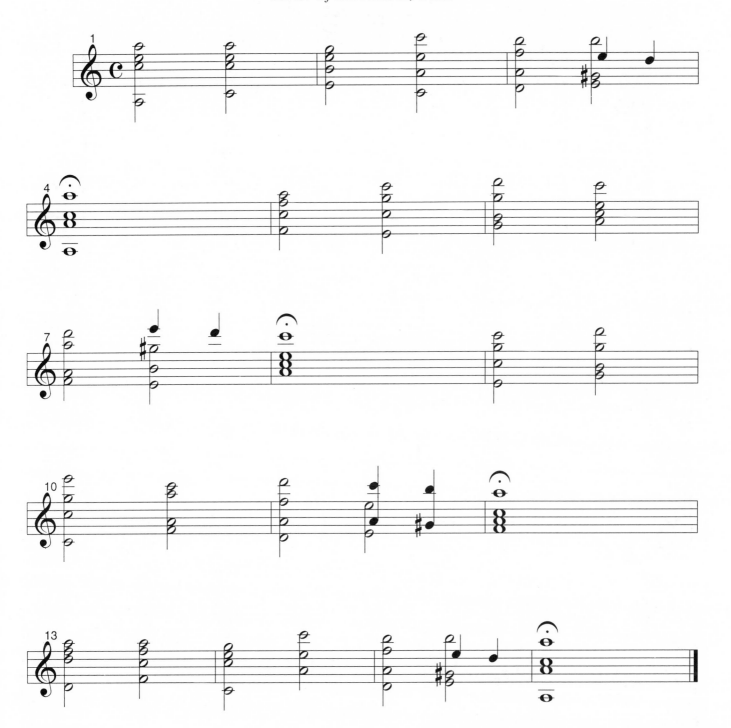

Bach Chorale Number 29 (Quartet)

"Help Us, Lord, In Our Endeavors"

Bach Chorale Number 29 (Trio)

"Help Us, Lord, In Our Endeavors"

Bach Chorale Number 29 (Duet)

"Help Us, Lord, In Our Endeavors"

Bach Chorale Number 29 (Melody Study)

"Help Us, Lord, In Our Endeavors"

Bach Chorale Number 29 (Bass Study)

"Help Us, Lord, In Our Endeavors"

Bach Chorale Number 29 (Solo)

"Help Us, Lord, In Our Endeavors"

181

Bach Chorale Number 30 (Quartet)

"In Thee, Lord, have I Put My Trust"

Bach Chorale Number 30 (Trio)

"In Thee, Lord, have I Put My Trust"

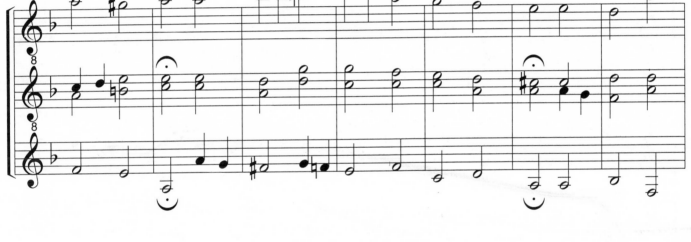

Bach Chorale Number 30 (Duet)

"In Thee, Lord, have I Put My Trust"

Bach Chorale Number 30 (Melody Study)

"In Thee, Lord, have I Put My Trust"

Bach Chorale Number 30 (Bass Study)

"In Thee, Lord, have I Put My Trust"

Bach Chorale Number 30 (Solo)

"In Thee, Lord, have I Put My Trust"

Bach Chorale Number 31 (Quartet)

"Jesus, I Will Never Leave"

188

Bach Chorale Number 31 (Trio)

"Jesus, I Will Never Leave"

Bach Chorale Number 31 (Duet)

"Jesus, I Will Never Leave"

Bach Chorale Number 31 (Melody Study)

"Jesus, I Will Never Leave"

Bach Chorale Number 31 (Bass Study)

"Jesus, I Will Never Leave"

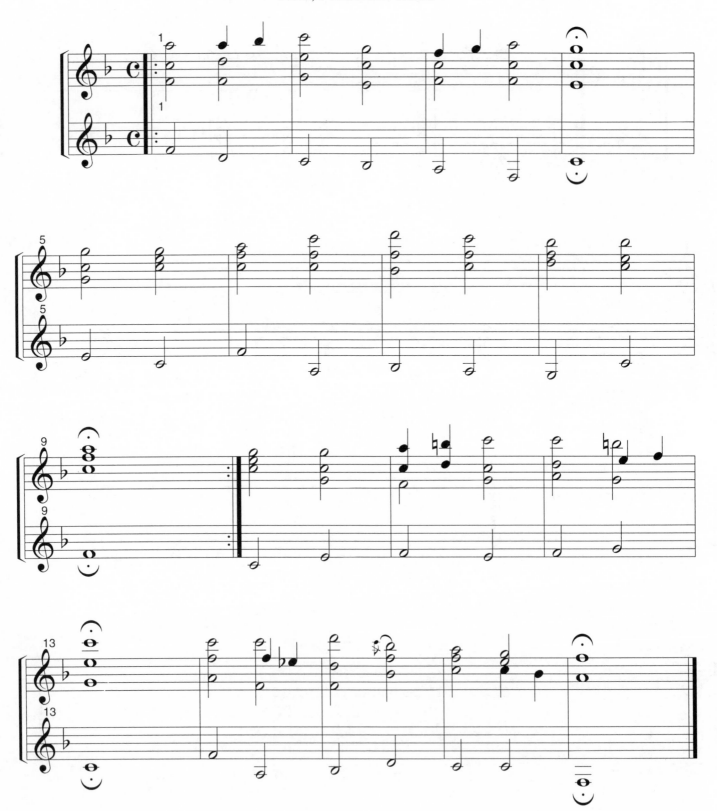

Bach Chorale Number 31 (Solo)

"Jesus, I Will Never Leave"

Bach Chorale Number 32 (Quartet)

"Our Father, Thou In Heav'n Above"

Bach Chorale Number 32 (Trio)

"Our Father, Thou In Heav'n Above"

Bach Chorale Number 32 (Duet)

"Our Father, Thou In Heav'n Above"

Bach Chorale Number 32 (Melody Study)

"Our Father, Thou In Heav'n Above"

Bach Chorale Number 32 (Bass Study)

"Our Father, Thou In Heav'n Above"

Bach Chorale Number 32 (Solo)

"Our Father, Thou In Heav'n Above"

Bach Chorale Number 33 (Quartet)

"If God Were Not Upon Our Side"

Bach Chorale Number 33 (Trio)

"If God Were Not Upon Our Side"

Bach Chorale Number 33 (Duet)

"If God Were Not Upon Our Side"

Bach Chorale Number 33 (Melody Study)

"If God Were Not Upon Our Side"

Bach Chorale Number 33 (Bass Study)

"If God Were Not Upon Our Side"

Bach Chorale Number 33 (Solo)

"If God Were Not Upon Our Side"

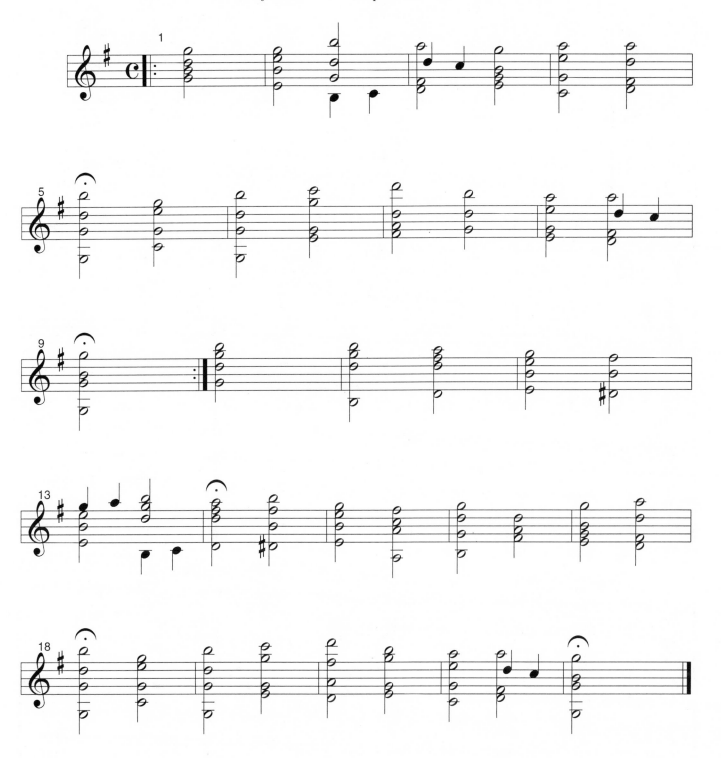

Bach Chorale Number 34 (Quartet)

"Both Life And Death Are Kept By Thee"

Bach Chorale Number 34 (Trio)

"Both Life And Death Are Kept By Thee"

Bach Chorale Number 34 (Duet)

"Both Life And Death Are Kept By Thee"

Bach Chorale Number 34 (Melody Study)

"Both Life And Death Are Kept By Thee"

Bach Chorale Number 34 (Bass Study)

"Both Life And Death Are Kept By Thee"

Bach Chorale Number 34 (Solo)

"Both Life And Death Are Kept By Thee"

Appendix

Duquesne University's Classical Guitar Department uses and strongly recommends the Aaron Shearer guitar methods from Mel Bay Publications.

It is an honor and true pleasure having Dr. Shearer as a member of our guitar faculty at Duquesne University's School of Music. Our students have gained insights and tremendous improvement in their performance levels by using Dr. Shearer's techniques as illustrated in his methods and through personal instruction with Aaron. His methods are complete in scope and establish all the essentials for masterful performance of the classic guitar. These books are an important part of my personal guitar library and should be studied by classic guitarists everywhere and at all levels of development.

Bill Purse
Chair Guitar, Duquesne University School of Music

Learning the Classic Guitar Part 1
by Aaron Shearer

CAT.#94361
BOOK $12.95

"Learning the Classic Guitar *is a new direction for guitar instruction. Many ideas in these books challenge traditional methods and assumptions.... In developing these books, I have adhered to the following concepts:*

*How and what students practice is as important as how much they practice.

*Give information only when it is immediately useful.

*Start with the easiest skills.

*Approach challenging skills gradually.

Over the years I have met a wide variety of talented people, many of whom have inspired me to develop a more effective approach to teaching the guitar. Through Learning the Classic Guitar, *I hope to share these advances."*

Mel Bay Publications is honored to present this authoritative and innovative series by Aaron Shearer, America's "Dean of the Classic Guitar."

Part 1 focuses on technical development and explains the most efficient approach to study and practice.

Learning the Classic Guitar Part 2
by Aaron Shearer

CAT.#94362
BOOK $14.95

Presents the elements of music and procedures for developing ability to sightread and memorize. It also introduces the visualization concept. *Part 1 and Part 2 are meant to be used simultaneously.*

Learning the Classic Guitar Part 3
by Aaron Shearer

CAT.#94363P
BOOK/CASSETTE PACKAGE $18.95

Teaches the student to form clear and accurate concepts of music expression. It also teaches the guitarist how to perform in public with accuracy and confidence.

If you have a sequencer, you can use it as a study partner!

Mel Bay Publications is offering the Bach chorales contained in this work as standard MIDI files.

Standard MIDI sequencer files are available for all thirty-four chorales, and each of the four voices may be auditioned or disabled for play-back at any tempo without changing their pitch. These sequences will allow you to play along with all the Bach chorale arrangements whether duo, trio, or quartet. You can play along with the computer for the solo chorales to check pitch and tempo accuracy in your performance. Each sequence includes all four voices (soprano, alto, tenor, and bass) on tracks one to four respectively. Track five contains a count-off rim shot on MIDI channel ten. Each track has the general MIDI patch change number for classical guitar, but you may experiment with reorchestrating by inserting whatever patch change numbers you wish. Please specify the type of computer platform you are using—Macintosh or IBM—when ordering.

ORDER FORM

Quantity

_____ 95050MMD Bach Chorales MIDI disk (Macintosh) $10.95

_____ 95050IMD Bach Chorales MIDI disk (IBM) 10.95

_____ 95050C Bach Chorales audio cassette 9.98

> **Please include postage & handling:**
> *$2.50 for 1 to 3 items*
> *$3.00 for 4 to 6 items*
> *$4.00 for 7 to 12 items*
> **You will be billed at standard rates for postage & handling on more than 12 items.**

Subtotal _____

Missouri Residents Add 6.225% Sales Tax _____

Add Postage & Handling _____

Total _____

No C.O.D. orders, please. Check, money order, or credit card information must accompany all orders.

Charge Cards: ☐ MasterCard ☐ Visa   Card Expires: Month _____ Year _____

Account Number: _____ Signature: _____

Name _____

Address _____

City _____ State _____ Zip _____

Telephone _____

MEL BAY PUBLICATIONS, INC.
#4 INDUSTRIAL DRIVE, PACIFIC, MO 63069-0066
Toll Free 1-800-8-MEL BAY (1-800-863-5229)   Fax 314-257-5062

DUQUESNE UNIVERSITY SCHOOL OF MUSIC

CLASSICAL AND CONTEMPORARY GUITAR AT DUQUESNE UNIVERSITY

WITH BILL PURSE, CHAIR GUITAR
DR. AARON SHEARER
AND TOM KIKTA

TE/GRADUATE DEGREES IN
EMPORARY GUITAR PERFORMANCE

EGREE AREAS INCLUDE
GY   MUSIC EDUCATION
ND SCIENCES   MUSIC THERAPY

• Pittsburgh, PA 15282-1803 • Phone (412) 396-6080

ASSISTANTSHIPS AVAILABLE •